No part of this book may be reproduced, or stored in a

retrieval system, or transmitted in any form or by any means,

electronic, mechanical, photocopying, recording, or

otherwise, without express written permission of the

publisher.

ISBN - 978-0-578-92243-0

Cover design by: Makinie (Soverall) Fortino

Printed in the United States of America

"Surely goodness and mercy shall follow me

all of the days of my life"

Psalms 23:6

This book is dedicated to all of the Matriarchs

in my family.

# Contents

# Foreword

Who am I? I am nothing without my people

(An Introduction to Makinie)

I am an Old Soul. I couldn't tell you about my past lives or age of my Spirit, but what I can tell you is that I was a precocious child who preferred nature to people and had grey hair and knee pain by age 13. I began to feel comfortable in my body when I turned 30, as though I grew into the age and body I was meant to be.

I am Black and Afro-Caribbean American -I write this because, while our spiritualities may be similar, there are SO MANY Black cultures, sometimes within one city or island, and when treating Black people, it is important to get a sense of what cultures we come from. We are incredibly diverse people. I am descended from West African people first and foremost, but share a connection with Latin America, Europe, India and the Indigenous of the Caribbean (specifically Arawak), that includes food, cultures AND spiritual practices.

I am my mother's daughter—wild at heart, lover of nature and possess a deep reverence for family, both past and present. My mom followed her calling, thereby teaching me how to do the same. She is my heroine and inspiration.

I am the granddaughter of Gramma Aurora and Gramma Emelda (may they rest in peace), who were graceful, creative, take-no-shit, straight-shooter women. One would not ask them for the truth or to talk about their feelings, unless they were prepared for a straightforward response, and wisdom.

I am the daughter of my father who taught me that to love is also to forgive and set healthy boundaries. His creativity lends to my own.

I am the older sister of two amazing siblings who followed me into the world of healing, but also chose their own paths. My brother has worked in a hospital and schools, and my sister taught preschool and is now studying to be a Nurse. When people look at us, they think I am the youngest, not because of how I look, but because of how wise they both are.

I am the wife of Brandon Fortino. To summarize our relationship in a nutshell, the first dance song we chose for our wedding was Spice and Wolf's season 1 opening song. Spice and Wolf is an anime about a traveling merchant who takes to the road with his Spirit Guide (in human form). This is an over-simplification of their story and ours, but hopefully you can understand the inferred parallels.

I am a BLERD (that means Black Nerd). I love all things Anime and Manga.

Much like many of my family members who held many roles and even more ideas, I work full-time as a counselor, own a private practice, am the President and Founder of DMHS and now, an author. It *almost* feels like I can never have too many careers.

I introduced myself to you in this particular way to demonstrate the African-Caribbean-American value system: We value storytelling, community, family, spirituality and finally, career. When people from the West introduce themselves, they ask "What do you do for a living?" When Black people are being introduced to one another, we ask "Who are your people?" "How is your family?".

# Orientation

The American Counseling Association defines Ethics under the ACA Code of Ethics as 'standards for counselors with the purpose of protecting the wellbeing of clients'. The Webster definition is 'moral principles that govern behavior', so please take this information to assess your moral principles and improve how you work with Black people and assess Black Mental Health, as my intention is to improve the treatment Black people receive from Mental Health & Wellness Professionals.

# Black Bodies Acknowledgement

I write because hundreds of thousands of Black voices were stolen. I also acknowledge that there are thousands of victims in the mental health system that have been crying out for compassion and help for decades, and that voices like mine are necessary, because theirs go unheard. I think anyone can be an activist, and everyone has a gift to offer. If I can help people look at the Black Experience in America a little differently, I can cause ripples. This manual is for the future Black lives, who you, the reader may look at with more context and compassion. If you are a mental health & wellness professional reading this, my hope is that your treatment approach is modified for improved mental health outcomes for Black people.

# Black Trauma: RBTS, PTSS, RBF

What we are witnessing in our offices or through our computer screens in sessions are descendants of West Africans who were kidnapped from their homeland, stuffed into ships like sardines, separated from their families and sold all over the South of USA, and Caribbean and enslaved by white people, then barred from opportunities, drugged, experimented on and overly-incarcerated, and all of the ways they are attempting to heal.

I will provide some examples of the various layers that contribute to the current state of racial trauma:

- Diagnoses during slavery such as 'Draptomania' and 'Negritude', which attempted to normalize slavery while demonizing dark skin of enslaved Africans.

- Dr. Sim's torture of enslaved Africans, especially Anarcha, Lucy and Betsy

- Oklahoma City Bombing

- Tuskegee Experiment

- Jim Crow

- The New Jim Crow (School to Prison Pipeline, and Mass Incarceration)

- 5,500 Lynchings between1877 and 1950

- The Tulsa Race Massacre, and the end of Black Wall Street

- Police Shootings

- Red Lining

These are just to name a few of many, which do not include what Black people currently face in the workplace, their neighborhoods, and schools, daily.

This is more of an intermediate manual, as many mental health professionals are more informed about racial trauma, and its symptoms, but I want to do a brief review while honoring the researchers and founders of these diagnoses, and I do consider them diagnoses, even not recognized by western mental health associations or councils.

**Dr. Robert T Carter** studied the impact of **Race-Based Traumatic Stress (RBTS)** and discrimination in the workplace. He determined in his studies that Black people exhibited symptoms of trauma directly related to how they were treated.

**Dr. William Smith** defined **Racial Battle Fatigue (RBF)** as a "cumulative result of a natural race-related stress response to distressing mental and emotional conditions. These conditions emerged from constantly facing racially dismissive, demeaning, insensitive and/or hostile racial environments and individuals."

**Dr. Joy DeGruy** said **Post Traumatic Slave Syndrome (PTSS)** was a result of **M.A.P**:

'M: Multigenerational trauma together with continued oppression.

A: Absence of opportunity to heal or access the benefits available in the society; leads to

P: Post Traumatic Slave Syndrome."

# West African Spirituality

Black people are constantly pulled away from our calling. When we are little, children make fun of us for our complexion, 'weird' names, big lips and coily hair. Sometimes to adapt, we adopt nicknames or abbreviated names to half-heartedly assimilate, while quietly wishing we could just fit in. Some of us even mistake this for wanting to be anything but Black. But sooner or later, the very features we are told are ugly, call us home and give us purpose. We learn to love our skin, hair, lips and names.

Many of us were raised in a way where tradition felt strange compared to what we saw in school, so many of our parents tried to make sure we were Americanized to have a better chance than they did, but also want to leave us with something to pass onto the next generation. One of the easiest ways to pass on tradition goes back to my introduction: food. Many of our families cook with a lot of things tied to spirituality—common household items then become our connection to our families and spiritual practices.

When we were enslaved and got sick, and were denied health care, we used herbs from our kitchens and prayers from our Ancestors, and accepted guidance from the indigenous of the Caribbean, South America, and North America. We also borrowed some aspects of our spirituality from Europeans (or rather, it was imposed, and we use what is beneficial to us, now). We embedded our cultures and traditions into American & Western religious belief systems, for survival, literally.

We trust the land and herbs before we turn to western medicine, and for obvious historical & present reasons, but also because we have been using our own remedies for so long. When we were denied health care and abused by doctors and psychologists, we began to turn to our families, communities, and churches.

Many of us also believe in "all things seen and unseen", and that belief is expressed in the form of traditional religions (Protestant, Catholicism, Christianity, Lutheranism, etc) , and African-Caribbean-American spiritual practices and/or religions such as Rootwork, Hoodoo, Rastafari, Haitian Voodoo, West African Vodun, and almost all of these are founded in our Ancestors' beliefs in "The Creator" , and deities that control elements such as rain, sun, wind, hurricanes.

# West African Spirituality in Western Society

Around 90% of Black American adults believe in a higher power. As I mentioned in the Foreword, many African, African American and Caribbean people are deeply religious, many *only* believe in God and practice Protestant, Catholicism, Christianity, Lutheran religions, or are Baptist or Jehovah's Witness. Others incorporate Afro Spirituality into their religions. Many opt out of religion, and practice Afro Spirituality *only*. There are those of African descent who practice Eastern religions like Buddhism, and finally, those who identify as atheist (around 3% of Black Americans).

Among many Black cultures, there are various approaches to spirituality and religion. Prior to colonization and the establishment of Christianity and Islam in West Africa, many of our spiritualities acknowledged an omnipotent being whom we call "The Creator" "Supreme God" "Creator Absolute God", in addition, many of our cultures and ethnic groups believe in 'lesser gods' who walk among us to guide us.

Some of these higher beings and gods come in the form of animal guides and/or can shapeshift. Indigenous here in North America and the Caribbean call them Spirit Animals, and in many west African-influenced cultures, we call them Spirit Guides.

Many African descendants in America have preserved some of these beliefs and traditions. A practice that many of us have in common, regardless of which religion or spiritual system we believe in is called Ancestor veneration. Ancestor veneration is the act of talking to and/or honoring Ancestors with things that they like. One example is leaving a plate of their favorite food or drink on an Ancestor Altar.

Some practice Ancestor and family veneration without realizing it. As an example, many Black people pour alcohol on the ground before consuming it nowadays, and that is directly tied to various traditions and cultures from Africa, which made their way to America and the Caribbean, that is called 'pouring libations'.

So, why am I telling you this? Because honoring Ancestors is connected to another part of our culture, which is experiencing 'gifts', and I will provide some examples under the Spiritual Awakening section.

Another thing many of us believe is that life does not end with death. Many of us continue to communicate with our loved ones who cross over, and some of us believe that there are Ancestors 'assigned to' us, to walk us through life. This does not mean that we do not grieve, but that in addition to grieving the physical loss, we acknowledge a spiritual gain. You may find that some of us may appear "less emotional" or sway between joy and weeping. In some of our cultures, (think, New Orleans and parts of the Caribbean), many of us don't even wear black to mourn, or to funerals— we wear the favorite color(s) of our loved ones, instead.

In pop culture, both The Lion King and Black Panther feature Ancestor veneration, and what some call 'council meetings' with Ancestors through visions or dreams, The Princess and the Frog feature a Voodoo priestess and a charlatan who claims to have access to hoodoo and voodoo. It also features animal and insect spirit guides. Finally, many of us believe that when we die, those of us who choose not to guide family may choose to return (reincarnation).

**Here is what encountering African Spiritualty may look like in a session:**

Clients may say things such as "I heard a voice that sounded like a relative that is dead," or "I'm channeling the energy of my grandmother". They may ask if you know anything about manifesting. They may share some of their experiences with communicating with loved ones who crossed over through tools like mirrors, dreams, fire, water or tarot. They might want to share some of their cultural practices, if they are comfortable enough. It's important to have some of this basic knowledge, so that when (not if) it comes up, you don't misinterpret these moments of openness and vulnerability with hallucinations or delusions.

As mental health & wellness practitioners, I believe it is our place to actively and non-judgmentally listen, then encourage, teach and review grounding activities and shadow work. This accomplishes a few things: Clients feel safe to discuss & explore their cultural practices, clients are in a space mentally, emotionally, and physically to engage in their practices in a safe way, AND may even positively impact their family and friends by normalizing these practices and traditions.

• • •

Because White people who enslaved our Ancestors tried to beat, guilt and shame African spirituality out of us, we embedded our culture into various religions. If you walk into a Black American or Caribbean home, you may see photos on the wall of Ancestors and biblical figures, bibles on tables with white cloths and candles, and maybe even an Ancestor Altar.

### Signs of Spiritual Awakenings:

- Imaginary friends (this occurs in childhood)

- Seeing spirit guides, Ancestors, or visitors in the house (ghosts)

- Hearing voices of spirit guides, Ancestors, or visitors in the house

- Past Life experiences (dreams, memories, or connection with heirlooms)

- Bodily sensations (Synesthesia, tingling sensations on scalp or over body)

- Insomnia

- Migraines

- Sensitivity to light and sound

- Dietary /appetite changes (usually loss of appetite, or transitioning from carnivore to pescatarian, vegetarian or vegan)

- Premonitions

- Ears ringing

27

- The ability to communicate with spirit guides or Ancestors through elements such as fire, mirrors, tea leaves or tarot cards

I know someone is reading this and thinking "but what if a Black person really is paranoid schizophrenic?", just as an example of what one may think while reading this list. I will tell you I have met dozens who were mis-diagnosed, and only a small few who actually experienced schizophrenia or delusions, by DSM and ICD criteria. According to The Rutgers University, Black people are 17 times more likely to be MID-diagnosed with Schizophrenia. It is not AS COMMON as we have been led to believe, in part because of implicit bias present in therapy sessions, as well as lack of culturally relevant context into Black Mental Health. Make sure to screen for diagnoses, but with the foundation that I, and many are providing regarding spirituality and racial trauma.

# Approaching Black Mental Health with Cultural Relevancy

### Diagnosis & Treatment Considerations:

We know that Racial Battle Fatigue, Racial Trauma and Post Traumatic Slave Syndrome will not be found in the DSM and ICD 10. So, my question is, how are you proceeding with Clients of Color and Black clients who clearly present with symptoms of these diagnoses that are not acknowledged? How are you documenting or justifying the diagnoses that you are using instead?

With regards to mis-diagnosis, one of the biggest contributing factors, aside from implicit bias is unfamiliarity with Afro-Caribbean-American Spirituality, and I have seen diagnoses and/or phrases in mental status exams such as "hypnopompic, hypnogogic, thought disorder, hallucination, magical thinking, perseveration, delusion, schizophrenia or angry", and we all know what happens when the medical community diagnoses Black people with delusions or schizophrenia.

I am not saying "don't diagnose" or "don't observe behaviors", but I am encouraging you to continue to build context through culturally relevant education and use an anti-racist checklist I provide below to explore a 'why/why not' of the diagnoses and adjectives you give, and what treatment modalities you will use.

**Anti-Racist Checklist:**

- How are you decolonizing your business?

- How are you using your MSE (Mental Status Exam)

- If you are diagnosing, are you also using V Codes?

- When using evidenced-based approaches, are you
  checking for implicit-bias or cultural relevancy?

- Are you actively seeking and learning from Black,
  Indigenous, POC, LGBTQIA, and immigrants?

- Is there diversity in your business?

- Are you living up to your logo or business title? (e.g.
  'Lotus Healing Hands')

- How are you incorporating non-
  Westernized/Colonized works into your practice?

- How are you using images on your website?

❑ How are you interacting with Black, Indigenous, POC, LGBTQIA and immigrants in therapy consult groups online or in person?

❑ What books are you recommending to your clients? What homework do you assign? Are they harmful?

❑ Are you crediting art and quotes when you use them on social media?

**Toolbox & Therapeutic Approaches**

**Recommendations:**

These are ways to ethically incorporate Afro-Spirituality into your practice, without committing cultural appropriation

- Encouraging/emphasizing the benefits of rest & self-care
- Including questions about impact of Racial Trauma in intake screening
- Making your space safe to allow Clients to talk about African-American-Caribbean spirituality openly
- Grounding skills / activities such as meditation and earthing
- Somatic Work
- Encouraging clients to build autonomy & self-trust through intuitive decision-making
- Systems Theory

- Shadow Work (e.g. Jung, journaling, exploring shame & triggers)
- Teaching self-advocacy
- Differentiation
- Music Therapy
- Helping client build support-system/community
- Helping client talk to family and friends about mental health (intergenerational repair & healing)
- Timely & appropriate self-disclosure
- EMDR

**Resources:**

These resources below is that they are from the perspective of and created by Black, Biracial & Indigenous people, and they use storytelling as a means of guiding healing.

**Book Recommendations for understanding and treating Racial Trauma:**

- Trauma Stewardship by Laura van Dernoot Lipsky, Connie Burk
- Post Traumatic Slave Syndrome by Dr. Joy DeGruy
- My Grandmother's Hands by Resmaa Menakem MSW
- Grieving While Black by Breeshia Wade
- Black Battle Fatigue in Higher Education by Kenneth J. Fasching-Varner, Forward by William A. Smith

- Measuring the Effects of Racism by Dr. Robert T. Carter

- The Four Agreements by Don Miguel Ruiz

**YouTube Keyword Searches:**

- "Black Affirmations"

- "Black Trauma Racial Trauma"

- "Black Male Grief"

- "Black Yoga"

- "Black Ted Talks"

- "Black Spirituality"

**Movie & Book recommendations to gain insight into themes of African-Caribbean-American Spirituality:**

- The Princess and the Frog

- The Lion King

- Black Panther

- Boyz-In-The-Hood

- Soul Food

- The Color Purple

- Children of Blood and Bone

- Daughters of the Dust

- Beyoncé: Lemonade

- Beyoncé: Black is King

- Eve's Bayou

**Non-Black films that explore similar themes:**

- Coco

- Moana

# Activism and Practicing Allyship,

# If One Is So Inclined

### DMHS: Deconstructing the Mental Health System, Inc, a (501)(c)(3) Nonprofit

The process of obtaining and maintaining my license, as well as a series of socio-political issues brought me to the point of realizing that intervening in systemic racism on an individual level was not enough. I decided that I wanted to start publicly pooling resources together, at no cost to those providing services, or those seeking services. Our main objective is to help Black and IPOC Therapists and Organizations advertise their services for free, as well as help those seeking services get information for free. We also list Free CEU opportunities. You can find out more information about what we are doing at https://dmhsus.org/

**How you can support DMHS:**

- Donate (specifically, allies)

- Add our BIPOC Provider listing to your website

- Share our BIPOC Provider listing with BIPOC mental health practitioners looking for free advertising

- Follow & share our social media, FB group for professionals & more: https://linktr.ee/dmhs

**Using The Power That You Have Within Your Organizations:**

- PAY BIPOC FOR OUR LABOR

- Give BIPOC Opportunities to share our ideas and tools

- Hire BIPOC speakers

**Using Your Personal Power:**

- Give free/reduced lease for office space

- Recommend BIPOC for leadership opportunities

- HIRE BIPOC for leadership positions

- Intervene/speak up in online groups and in person when injustice is occuring

- Take what you learn and teach it to colleagues, friends, and family

- Donate to BIPOC-lead causes

# In Closing

I hope that you have enjoyed this (very) brief manual. The information provided in this is a drop in an ocean compared to work that needs to be done but will be a good foundation to begin doing the work and research that needs to be done to provide TRULY equitable service or build on it. My intention is for you to take the information here and expand your research, be it looking into racial trauma assessments, or researching Afro spirituality more in-depth.

If you are non-Black, I discourage you from turning to your Black friends or family members, or colleagues to ask about this, because as I stated in the very beginning, "Black Culture" is a term that encompasses an immeasurable level of diversity, and quite frankly, information is readily available via online search or videos.

I hope this is the beginning of a journey for you, that Black clients benefit from and can experience improved mental health treatment.

Thank you for reading this manual.

# About the Author

**Makinie (Soverall) Fortino**

(https://linktr.ee/MakinieTherapy) identifies as Black and

Afro-Caribbean American and is a Licensed Marriage and

Family Therapist (LMFT) who has been working in mental

health for 9 years. Makinie has worked for State of

Washington for the last few years, most recently as a

Behavioral Health Counselor at Renton Technical College.

Makinie also owns a Private Practice and founded DMHS: Deconstructing the Mental Health System, Inc to bring anti-racist therapists together to address the mental health system's racial and financial inequities, through education and other initiatives, such as a free provider listing for BIPOC Therapists. Makinie's Private Practice, the founding of DMHS and even this book was created out of the need to feel more grounded in holistic counseling as well as continued dedication to systemic change to our current mental health system on both individual and collective levels.

# Notes & Citation:

I have cited all of my sources, to the best of my ability in earnestness.

- DRAPETOMANIA --- A DISEASE CALLED FREEDOM (archive.org)

  https://web.archive.org/web/20090215004923/http:/www.broward.org/library/bienes/lii13000.htm

- An Early History - African American Mental Health (udayton.edu)

  https://academic.udayton.edu/health/01status/mental01.htm

- Depression or schizophrenia? Black patients more likely to be misdiagnosed)

  https://www.mentalhealthtoday.co.uk/news/awareness/depression-or-schizophrenia-black-patients-more-likely-to-be-misdiagnosed#:~:text=About%20600%20were%20African%20American,as%20schizophrenia%20or%20bipolar%20disorder.

- J. Marion Sims: The 'Father Of Gynecology' Who Experimented On Slaves (allthatsinteresting.com)

  https://allthatsinteresting.com/j-marion-sims

- The New Orleans Medical And Surgical Journal : Free Download, Borrow, and Streaming : Internet Archive

  https://archive.org/details/TheNewOrleansMedicalAndSu rgicalJournal/mode/1up?view=theater

- The historical roots of racial disparities in the mental health system - Counseling Today

  https://ct.counseling.org/2020/05/the-historical-roots-of-racial-disparities-in-the-mental-health-system/

- Why Mental Health Care is Stigmatized in Black Communities | USC Social Work

  https://dworakpeck.usc.edu/news/why-mental-health-care-stigmatized-black-communities

- Advocates for LGBT youth call for ending "school-to-prison" pipeline - Metro Weekly

  https://www.metroweekly.com/2015/09/advocates-for-lgbt-youth-call-for-ending-school-to-prison-pipeline/

46

- Black Lives Matter: Anti-Racism Resources for Social Workers and Therapists - SocialWork.Career

  https://www.socialwork.career/2020/06/anti-racism-resources-for-social-workers-and-therapists.html

- RTCA (rtca411.com)

  https://www.rtca411.com/

- African Americans Have Limited Access to Mental and Behavioral Health Care (apa.org)

  https://www.apa.org/advocacy/civil-rights/diversity/african-american-health

- (30) "Black Male Grief Reactions to Race-Based Traumatic Losses Among Emerging Adult Black Men" – YouTube

  https://www.youtube.com/watch?v=KzhV7Spwnl8

- U.S. Slavery: Timeline, Figures & Abolition – HISTORY

  https://www.history.com/topics/black-history/slavery

- Life Story: Anarcha, Betsy, and Lucy - Women & the American Story (nyhistory.org)

  https://wams.nyhistory.org/a-nation-divided/antebellum/anarcha-betsy-lucy/

- POST TRAUMATIC SLAVE SYNDROME — Dr. Joy
  DeGruy

  https://www.joydegruy.com/post-traumatic-slave-
  syndrome

- ACA Code of Ethics

  https://www.counseling.org/Resources/aca-code-of-
  ethics.pdf

- Faith Among Black Americans

  https://www.pewforum.org/2021/02/16/faith-among-
  black-americans/

- Racial and Ethnic Composition

  https://www.pewforum.org/religious-landscape-
  study/racial-and-ethnic-composition/black/

Made in the USA
Coppell, TX
27 July 2021